RING TO REMEMBER

A HEAVEN'S BELL GRIEF JOURNAL AND MEMORY BOOK

SHERRIE BARCH

Copyright © 2022 Sherrie Barch All rights reserved.

All rights reserved. In accordance with the U.S. Copyright Act of 1976, the scanning, uploading, and electronic sharing of any part of this book without the permission of the publisher is unlawful piracy and theft of the author's intellectual property. Please purchase only authorized editions, and do not participate in or encourage electronic piracy of copyrighted materials. If you would like to use material from this book (other than for review purposes), prior written permission must be obtained by contacting the publisher at sherrie@heavensbell.com

Thank you for your support of this author's rights.

Although every precaution has been taken to verify the accuracy of the information contained herein, the author and publisher assume no responsibility for any errors or omissions. No liability is assumed for damages that may result from the use of information contained within.

Project Management: Shannon Oakes, www.creativeapogee.com

Cover: Sabrina Peregolise Telis

Inside Layout: Ljilijana Pavkov

Printed in the United States of America

FIRST EDITION

Library of Congress

ISBN: 978-1-7362638-2-2 (international trade paper edition)

For Ray Smith and Richard Barch

Introduction:

After releasing my book, Heaven's Bell in 2020, I learned so much about how others experience and express grief. I found that while the need for a story readers could relate to was important, the greater need was for a safe space to process that grief while coping with the death of a loved one.

Each time I asked someone what they thought of Heaven's Bell, the response was immediately about their loved one instead of the book. It seems that reading Ashley and Cody's story of love, eternal friendship, and grieving is the entryway to the path that many readers are seeking to share their own feelings.

This entire journey to Heaven's Bell and the journal you now hold began in 2016 when I wrote a page and a half essay called "Your Heaven's Bell" while staying at a lakeside cabin. I felt a push to share the story of how everyone has their own "heaven's bell" that is hung in the Great Hall when they die and rings when a loved one on Earth remembers them.

The Ring To Remember Journal is the newest addition to the emotional safe space to grieve, originally created by the book. It is also a direct response to the voices of my readers and their touching book reviews, where they have shared stories, opinions of the book, and also the raw and deeply personal emotions they experienced while reading the book. Through their beautiful words they have, in a sense, requested a broader space to remember and write about loved ones who have passed.

This journal is that space.

In these pages, you have a space to reflect on your loved one who is no longer with you, your memories with them, your vision of heaven (or your version of that word as this is meant to be a nondenominational story), and the lessons you have learned from loss.

Whether you answer the prompts in order, or by choosing the one that is currently tugging at your soul, there is no wrong way to navigate this journal. This is your space - do what feels right for you. It is laid out so that you can express yourself in any way you see fit - writing, doodling, drawing, attaching photos or momentos. I encourage you to truly make it your own.

If this journal has found you before the book itself, I invite you to get your copy of *Heaven's Bell* at www.heavensbell.com.

And when you're done, or even while you're still navigating the prompts, you can connect with the community of other *Heaven's Bell* and *Ring To Remember* readers like yourself. Please visit www.ringtorememberjournal.com and share your reading and journaling experiences. I look forward to seeing you there!

RING TO REMEMBER

My grief journal and memory book for

....

Close your eyes and picture your loved one. Describe or draw how you remember them.

....
....
....
....
....

What are they wearing?

....
....
....

Where do you see them?

....
....
....

What are they doing?

....
....
....

What are they saying?

....
....
....

This is a space to doodle, draw, tape, glue, write, express feelings, and share memories in your own way.

What are the first three words that come to mind when you think of your loved one?

Why these words?

This is a space to doodle, draw, tape, glue, write, express feelings, and share memories in your own way.

Describe your loved one's personality.

Did they remind you of anyone?

What personality traits did they share with you or other family members?

This is a space to doodle, draw, tape, glue, write, express feelings, and share memories in your own way.

What was your loved one's favorite piece of clothing?

....
....
....
....
....

Describe it in as much detail as possible.

....
....
....
....
....

Do you know why it was a favorite?

....
....
....
....
....

Did they wear it everywhere or was it just for special occasions?

....
....
....
....
....

This is a space to doodle, draw, tape, glue, write, express feelings,
and share memories in your own way.

What is your keepsake or reminder of your loved one and why is it important to you?

....
....
....
....
....
....

Where do you keep it? Is it in a special place like a memory pillow, stuffed animal, keepsake box, etc?

....
....
....
....
....
....

Is it something you always keep on you or close to you or do you keep it safely stored away to take out only on special occasions?

....
....
....
....
....
....

This is a space to doodle, draw, tape, glue, write, express feelings, and share memories in your own way.

What was your loved one's favorite food?

What about dessert?

What meal would they choose for a birthday or other special day?

This is a space to doodle, draw, tape, glue, write, express feelings, and share memories in your own way.

Where was your loved one's favorite vacation spot or place they visited?

....
....
....
....
....

What stories, descriptions or information did your loved one share about their trip(s)?

....
....
....
....
....

Did you ever visit this place with them? If so, what are your memories?

....
....
....
....
....

If not, what would you do in memory of your loved one, or to honor them if you ever did visit there?

....
....
....
....
....

This is a space to doodle, draw, tape, glue, write, express feelings, and share memories in your own way.

What type of music did your loved one like?

....
....
....
....
....
....
....

What do you think is on their playlist in heaven? Create a playlist of their top 10 favorite songs and list them here.

....
....
....
....
....
....
....
....
....
....
....
....
....
....

This is a space to doodle, draw, tape, glue, write, express feelings, and share memories in your own way.

Did your loved one have a favorite place to just relax and enjoy some "me" time? Where was it and what did they do while there (read, draw, sing, listen to music, etc)?

....
....
....
....
....
....
....
....

Do you ever spend time in this place? If so, what do you do or think about while there?

....
....
....
....
....
....
....
....
....

This is a space to doodle, draw, tape, glue, write, express feelings, and share memories in your own way.

What was your loved one's favorite form of entertainment?
Did they enjoy TV, music, movies, books, live theater, or something else?
Write their favorites below:

Favorite books
....
....

Favorite TV shows
....
....

Favorite movies
....
....

Favorite actors
....
....

Favorite bands
....
....

Favorite musicals or plays
....
....

Other favorites
....
....

This is a space to doodle, draw, tape, glue, write, express feelings, and share memories in your own way.

If your loved one was described as the biggest fan of a team, event, cause, or something else, what would that be?

....
....
....
....
....
....

How did they show their support?

....
....
....
....
....
....

Did they collect anything or have any momentos to show their involvement? If so, describe the items and where they were kept/displayed.

....
....
....
....
....
....

This is a space to doodle, draw, tape, glue, write, express feelings, and share memories in your own way.

Did your loved one cook or make a special dish? If so, what was it?

....
....

Was it a family recipe or something that they made as part of a tradition? Does anyone make it now?

....
....

Are there any stories about traditions, gatherings, secret ingredients, etc. that are shared whenever someone makes it?

....
....
....
....
....
....
....
....
....
....
....

This is a space to doodle, draw, tape, glue, write, express feelings, and share memories in your own way.

What was your loved one's favorite restaurant?

....
....
....

Did they always order one thing or did they love the whole menu?

....
....
....

What special occasions did they celebrate at this restaurant?

....
....
....

What special memories do you have of them while at this restaurant?

....
....
....
....
....
....
....
....
....

This is a space to doodle, draw, tape, glue, write, express feelings, and share memories in your own way.

What was your loved one's favorite color?

....
....
....

Do you know why it was their favorite?

....
....
....
....
....
....
....

What items in this color remind you of them?

....
....
....
....
....
....
....
....
....

This is a space to doodle, draw, tape, glue, write, express feelings, and share memories in your own way.

Did your loved one like animals?

....
....
....

Did they have a favorite animal?

....
....
....

Did they have a favorite pet? Why was it their favorite?

....
....
....
....
....
....

Are there any special or funny stories your loved one shared about their pets or favorite animals?

....
....
....
....
....
....

This is a space to doodle, draw, tape, glue, write, express feelings, and share memories in your own way.

What was your loved one's favorite hobby?

....
....
....
....
....
....

Did you ever participate with them?

....
....
....
....
....
....

Why do you think they enjoyed this hobby?

....
....
....
....
....
....

This is a space to doodle, draw, tape, glue, write, express feelings,
and share memories in your own way.

Did your loved one have a nickname that others called them?

Was there a special nickname that only you had for them?

What's the story behind these nicknames?

This is a space to doodle, draw, tape, glue, write, express feelings, and share memories in your own way.

Did your loved one have a special nickname for you? What's the story behind it?

This is a space to doodle, draw, tape, glue, write, express feelings, and share memories in your own way.

In *Heaven's Bell* the illustrations are what the author imagines
the Great Hall and all its parts to look like.
How do you picture heaven?

....
....
....
....
....
....
....
....
....
....
....
....

Did your loved one ever share what they thought heaven would be like?

....
....
....
....
....
....
....

This is a space to doodle, draw, tape, glue, write, express feelings, and share memories in your own way.

**Do you think of the afterlife as "heaven" or as something else?
Write or draw what you think it would be like.**

This is a space to doodle, draw, tape, glue, write, express feelings, and share memories in your own way.

What do you imagine your loved one's "heaven's bell" looks like?

What do you think it sounds like?

How do you imagine your bell will look and sound?

This is a space to doodle, draw, tape, glue, write, express feelings, and share memories in your own way.

If your loved one could hang out with anyone in heaven, who do you think they would choose? Think of other family members, friends, even celebrities or heros! Anything is possible!

This is a space to doodle, draw, tape, glue, write, express feelings, and share memories in your own way.

Thinking of other family and friends who have died, what do you envision they are all doing in heaven?

....
....
....
....
....
....
....
....

What do you envision you will be doing once you arrive in heaven?

....
....
....
....
....
....
....
....
....

This is a space to doodle, draw, tape, glue, write, express feelings, and share memories in your own way.

Keeping a loved one alive in the hearts and minds of those who knew them can be done in many ways. It can be something as small as the ringing of a bell to show you are thinking of them or as big as a foundation or scholarship set up in their name. How do you honor your loved one?

This is a space to doodle, draw, tape, glue, write, express feelings, and share memories in your own way.

Of all your loved one's traits or skills, what were your favorites?

With that in mind, answer this question: If I could be like my loved one in any way, I would continue their ability to .... because

This is a space to doodle, draw, tape, glue, write, express feelings, and share memories in your own way.

When others ask you what happened to your loved one, what is the story you share about their death?

This is a space to doodle, draw, tape, glue, write, express feelings, and share memories in your own way.

If you could have one more conversation with your loved one, what would you discuss?

....
....
....
....
....
....
....
....
....

Would you ask questions about heaven, their life, your life, or something else entirely? What do you think they would say?

....
....
....
....
....
....
....
....
....
....

This is a space to doodle, draw, tape, glue, write, express feelings,
and share memories in your own way.

What do you want other people to know about your loved one?
Share a few memories or stories about what made your loved one special to you and to others.

This is a space to doodle, draw, tape, glue, write, express feelings, and share memories in your own way.

What season is the hardest without your loved one? Why that season in particular?

....
....
....
....
....
....
....
....

What can you do to honor their memory and make this an easier time?

....
....
....
....
....
....
....
....
....
....
....

This is a space to doodle, draw, tape, glue, write, express feelings, and share memories in your own way.

What are the top three emotions you feel when you think of your loved one? Write down each emotion and why you think that emotion shows up when you have thoughts of them.

This is a space to doodle, draw, tape, glue, write, express feelings, and share memories in your own way.

Our own senses can remind us of our loved ones who have died.
Write some examples of thoughts and memories of your loved one
that are triggered by the following senses:

Sight -

....
....
....

Smell -

....
....
....

Taste -

....
....
....

Sound -

....
....
....

Touch -

....
....
....

This is a space to doodle, draw, tape, glue, write, express feelings, and share memories in your own way.

We learn so many things from others in our lives.
What did you learn from your loved one that you are grateful for today?

This is a space to doodle, draw, tape, glue, write, express feelings,
and share memories in your own way.

Is there anything you wanted to do with your loved one that you never did?

Do you still plan to do it without them?

If so, what do you think the experience will be like and what would they do or say if they were able to take part?

This is a space to doodle, draw, tape, glue, write, express feelings, and share memories in your own way.

What do you remember about the last time you saw your loved one?

Where were you?

What was happening around you?

What did you and your loved one say or communicate to one another?

This is a space to doodle, draw, tape, glue, write, express feelings, and share memories in your own way.

If there was a way to send your loved one a gift in heaven, what would it be?

....
....
....

Why that specific gift?

....
....
....
....
....
....
....
....
....
....
....
....
....
....
....
....
....

This is a space to doodle, draw, tape, glue, write, express feelings, and share memories in your own way.

Do you share any traits with your loved one?

In what ways are you most like them?

In what ways are you different?

This is a space to doodle, draw, tape, glue, write, express feelings, and share memories in your own way.

What do you think your loved one's hopes are for your future?

....
....
....
....
....

Did you ever talk with them about major life decisions such as goals, relationships, school, or jobs??

....
....
....
....
....

Do you still have the same hopes and plans or have they changed now?

....
....
....
....
....

If so, what do you think your loved one would think of the changes?

....
....
....
....
....

This is a space to doodle, draw, tape, glue, write, express feelings,
and share memories in your own way.

What is the first thing you are going to say to your loved one when you see them in heaven?

What do you think they will say to you?

This is a space to doodle, draw, tape, glue, write, express feelings, and share memories in your own way.

Who are the people who help you remember your loved one's life?

....
....
....
....
....

Are there any stories others have shared since your loved one's death that help you remember them?

....
....
....
....
....

Is there a special story or memory everyone seems to tell about them over and over again?

....
....
....
....
....

This is a space to doodle, draw, tape, glue, write, express feelings, and share memories in your own way.

Are there certain items or objects that you associate with your loved one? Describe some of those special things and share why they remind you of them.

This is a space to doodle, draw, tape, glue, write, express feelings,
and share memories in your own way.

Aside from special occasions, are there other days that you find yourself thinking of and missing your loved one?

What are the ordinary routines you miss with them?

This is a space to doodle, draw, tape, glue, write, express feelings, and share memories in your own way.

Do you believe that you can receive messages or signs from your loved one in heaven?

....

....

How do you think those are sent? Do you get them through music, drama, art, smells, not-so-random objects that you see or find?

....

....

....

....

....

....

....

What messages do you think you've received from your loved one?

....

....

....

....

....

....

....

....

This is a space to doodle, draw, tape, glue, write, express feelings, and share memories in your own way.

Are your decisions in life guided by your relationship with your loved one?
If so, how do you use your loved one's influence to make your decisions?

This is a space to doodle, draw, tape, glue, write, express feelings, and share memories in your own way.

Is there someone that helps you get through the tougher times?

....
....
....
....
....
....

How do they help?

....
....
....
....
....
....

When are you most likely to need them?

....
....
....
....
....
....

This is a space to doodle, draw, tape, glue, write, express feelings, and share memories in your own way.

Facing life without someone we love is one of the hardest parts of death. What scares you the most about your loved one being gone?

What helps you get through those fears?

This is a space to doodle, draw, tape, glue, write, express feelings, and share memories in your own way.

What future events will you miss most without your loved one?

....
....
....
....
....
....
....
....

How will you honor their memory and carry them with you during those times?

....
....
....
....
....
....
....
....
....
....

This is a space to doodle, draw, tape, glue, write, express feelings, and share memories in your own way.

What do you wish people had told you about death before your loved one died?

....
....
....
....
....
....
....
....

How would this information have helped you deal with their death differently?

....
....
....
....
....
....
....
....
....
....

This is a space to doodle, draw, tape, glue, write, express feelings, and share memories in your own way.

What is one thing you can do on days when coping with your grief is really hard?

....
....
....
....
....
....
....
....
....
....
....

How does this help?

....
....
....
....
....
....
....
....
....
....
....

This is a space to doodle, draw, tape, glue, write, express feelings, and share memories in your own way.

What do you think your loved one would say to you when you're having a hard time coping with their death?

....
....
....
....
....
....
....
....
....
....

What would they tell you to do for others and say to others who are struggling with grief too?

....
....
....
....
....
....
....
....
....
....
....
....

This is a space to doodle, draw, tape, glue, write, express feelings, and share memories in your own way.

Is there a certain time when you feel most connected to your loved one (time of day, season, situations, etc.)?

....
....
....
....
....
....
....
....

Why are you more connected with them at these times?

....
....
....
....
....
....
....
....

This is a space to doodle, draw, tape, glue, write, express feelings, and share memories in your own way.

What does coping with the death of your loved one feel like?
What words would you use to describe these feelings?

How are you taking care of yourself and showing self compassion?

This is a space to doodle, draw, tape, glue, write, express feelings, and share memories in your own way.

Who did you first turn to when your loved one died?

Do you still go to them when you need comfort?

Where else do you find comfort?

This is a space to doodle, draw, tape, glue, write, express feelings, and share memories in your own way.

Life is always moving and changing, even when we are grieving. We meet new people and make new friends and of course, wish they could have known our loved one who died. Name three people you would like to introduce your loved one to and why.

....
....
....
....
....
....
....
....

What do you believe your loved one would have thought of them?

....
....
....
....
....
....
....
....
....

This is a space to doodle, draw, tape, glue, write, express feelings, and share memories in your own way.

Stories are the best way to remember those who have died. Ask others for stories of your loved one that you may not have heard before and write them here.

This is a space to doodle, draw, tape, glue, write, express feelings, and share memories in your own way.

Where did you see your loved one most of the time? Did you live together, was it at school or work or in the community or elsewhere?

....
....
....
....
....
....
....

What is it like being back in this place now?

....
....
....
....
....

If it's hard or painful, what could you do to make it easier to be there?

....
....
....
....
....

This is a space to doodle, draw, tape, glue, write, express feelings, and share memories in your own way.

If you could take a walk down Memory Lane with your loved one, what would you both see? Write three key memories you shared with them.

This is a space to doodle, draw, tape, glue, write, express feelings,
and share memories in your own way.

What piece of advice did your loved one share that you remember most?

....
....
....
....
....
....

Did you take their advice? If yes, are you still following it?

....
....
....
....
....
....

Do you share this advice with others? If so, who and why?

....
....
....
....
....
....

This is a space to doodle, draw, tape, glue, write, express feelings, and share memories in your own way.

Did your loved one have a catch phrase or saying that they were known for?

....
....
....
....
....
....
....
....
....

When you think of them and imagine their voice in your head, what are they most often saying?

....
....
....
....
....
....
....
....
....
....
....

This is a space to doodle, draw, tape, glue, write, express feelings, and share memories in your own way.

Was your loved one usually serious or were they often funny?

....
....
....
....
....
....

Was there ever a joke or funny story they told that made you laugh? What was it?

....
....
....
....
....
....

What was a joke or story you told your loved one that made them laugh?

....
....
....
....
....
....

This is a space to doodle, draw, tape, glue, write, express feelings,
and share memories in your own way.

What activities did you and your loved one share that brought you joy?

Do you still enjoy these activities?

When enjoying these activities now, what do you do the same and what do you do differently?

This is a space to doodle, draw, tape, glue, write, express feelings, and share memories in your own way.

What was your loved one's favorite holiday?

....
....
....
....
....

Why was it their favorite?

....
....
....
....
....

What were some of the traditions or activities they enjoyed during this holiday season?

....
....
....
....
....

What one thing reminds you the most of them during this holiday?

....
....
....
....
....

This is a space to doodle, draw, tape, glue, write, express feelings, and share memories in your own way.

What was a cause your loved one was passionate about?

....
....
....
....
....

Why was this so important to them?

....
....
....
....
....

What did they do to support this cause?

....
....
....
....
....

Do you do anything in their memory for this cause?

....
....
....
....
....

This is a space to doodle, draw, tape, glue, write, express feelings, and share memories in your own way.

What do you remember most about your loved one?

How did your loved one make you feel when you spent time together?

This is a space to doodle, draw, tape, glue, write, express feelings, and share memories in your own way.

List three ways you can celebrate your loved one's memory.

This is a space to doodle, draw, tape, glue, write, express feelings, and share memories in your own way.

What kind of everyday activities did your loved one do to help and give back to others?

....
....
....
....
....
....
....
....

What are three random acts of kindness you can do regularly to honor them?

....
....
....
....
....
....
....
....
....
....
....

This is a space to doodle, draw, tape, glue, write, express feelings, and share memories in your own way.

If you could tell your loved one about your day, what would you tell them (or if you could show them your day, what would you put on the monitors in the Great Hall)?

This is a space to doodle, draw, tape, glue, write, express feelings, and share memories in your own way.

Describe when you feel most connected to your loved one and "ring their bell."

This is a space to doodle, draw, tape, glue, write, express feelings, and share memories in your own way.

What was the most adventurous or scariest thing you and your loved one did together?

Why did you do it and how did you both feel afterwards?

This is a space to doodle, draw, tape, glue, write, express feelings, and share memories in your own way.

If you could pick an ideal place to spend an entire day with your loved one, where would you go?

What would be on your list of things to do while there?

What would you talk to your loved one about?

This is a space to doodle, draw, tape, glue, write, express feelings, and share memories in your own way.

What was the nicest thing your loved one did for you?

....
....
....
....
....
....
....
....

What was the nicest thing your loved one ever said to you?

....
....
....
....
....
....
....
....
....
....
....

This is a space to doodle, draw, tape, glue, write, express feelings, and share memories in your own way.

Did you and your loved one share an inside joke? If so, what was it and what's the story behind it?

....
....
....
....
....
....
....
....
....
....

Do you share this inside joke with anyone else now or is it still something just between you and your loved one?

....
....
....
....
....
....
....
....
....
....

This is a space to doodle, draw, tape, glue, write, express feelings, and share memories in your own way.

As you grieve, what have you learned about yourself so far?

How do you think the death of your loved one has affected you the most?

This is a space to doodle, draw, tape, glue, write, express feelings, and share memories in your own way.

What are some ways you can use your loss to help others who are experiencing grief too?

....
....
....
....
....
....
....
....
....

What one piece of advice would you give to someone who is grieving?

....
....
....
....
....
....
....
....
....
....

This is a space to doodle, draw, tape, glue, write, express feelings, and share memories in your own way.

Have you read the book, *Heaven's Bell*?
If so, how did the story help you grieve?

....
....
....
....
....
....

How would you describe your reading experience to others in this situation?

....
....
....
....
....

Who could you help by telling them the Heaven's Bell story?

....
....
....
....
....

This is a space to doodle, draw, tape, glue, write, express feelings, and share memories in your own way.

What have been the toughest parts of grief for you?

What help did you ask for and receive?

What advice would you share with others to help them get through the same challenges during their grieving process?

This is a space to doodle, draw, tape, glue, write, express feelings, and share memories in your own way.

Conclusion:

I hope your responses to the Ring To Remember prompts have helped you on your healing journey, and the experience of writing, drawing, collecting, taping, gluing, etc. provided a safe space for you to grieve and celebrate your loved one. Please continue to add to this journal anytime you hear new stories or think of additional memories.

Here are a few final questions for you:

How did Ring To Remember help you?

Where were you physically and emotionally when you began your journal, and where are you now?

What memories of your loved one are clearer and may be more lasting for you after answering the prompts in your journal?

How will you share your Heaven's Bell reading and Ring To Remember journaling experience with others who are grieving?

I encourage all of my readers and journal writers, like you, to share the inspirational and healing message of *Heaven's Bell* and *Ring To Remember* with as many people as possible. There are some really easy ways to do so. First, please share your copy of the book or gift a new journal and book to a friend or family member who may need comfort. Second, if you are aware of organizations, grief counseling centers, schools, hospices, or others that may benefit from the *Heaven's Bell* book and *Ring To Remember* journal, please contact me at sherrie@heavensbell.com. I want to help. And lastly, if you enjoyed the journal and/or the book, please leave a review on Amazon.

Finally, from the bottom of my heart, thank you for being a part of the Heaven's Bell community and supporting this little story I wrote that evening in 2016, sitting on the porch of a cabin, watching the sun set over the lake. The hundreds of beautiful stories told by readers are truly more meaningful than I could have ever wished for when I set out to share the story of *Heaven's Bell*. I am both humbled and grateful.

Ring To Remember,
Sherrie

About Sherrie Barch:

Sherrie Barch is the CEO of two Forbes' ranked top executive search firms and a leadership consulting company. An expert in the areas of leadership, team development, and diversity, her forward-thinking approach to work was recognized when she was chosen to participate in the 'altMBA" program designed and led by leadership guru Seth Godin. Born and raised in Northern Illinois, Sherrie earned Bachelor and Master of Arts degrees in Communication from Western Illinois University.

Sherrie is married with three sons. As a mom, she describes herself as a part-time pancreas for her two youngest sons who were both diagnosed with Type 1 Diabetes within the same year. Playing this role for several years now, she is relentless about creating open and honest communication with her family about this chronic and life-threatening condition.

Sherrie's passion for storytelling and making room for serious and "heavy" conversations was a strong motivation for her to write her children's book Heaven's Bell and its companion grief journal and memory book *Ring To Remember*. One of her goals for *Heaven's Bell* and the *Ring To Remember* journal is to create and inspire a safe space for families to share memories and have conversations about death and dying in a natural and productive way.

Sherrie is currently working on her second book, a business leadership fable designed to help new college graduates navigate the "real life stuff they don't teach you in school" about career conversations, conflicts, and challenges.

In her leisure time, she enjoys the changing seasons of the Midwest, spending time with her family and friends and live entertainment in any form including Broadway plays, school plays, comedians, magicians, and musicians.